THE
EXPECTATIONS
OF LIGHT

Princeton Series of Contemporary Poets
David Wagoner, *Editorial Adviser*

OTHER BOOKS IN THE SERIES
Returning Your Call, by Leonard Nathan
Sadness And Happiness, by Robert Pinsky
Burn Down the Icons, by Grace Schulman
Reservations, by James Richardson
The Double Witness, by Ben Belitt
Night Talk and Other Poems, by Richard Pevear
Listeners at the Breathing Place, by Gary Miranda
The Power to Change Geography, by Diana Ó Hehir
An Explanation of America, by Robert Pinsky
Signs and Wonders, by Carl Dennis
Walking Four Ways in the Wind, by John Allman
Hybrids of Plants and of Ghosts, by Jorie Graham
Movable Islands, by Deborah Greger
Yellow Stars and Ice, by Susan Stewart

Pattiann Rogers

The Expectations
of Light

PRINCETON
UNIVERSITY
PRESS

Published by Princeton University Press, Princeton, New Jersey
In the United Kingdom: Princeton University Press, Guildford, Surrey

All Rights Reserved

Library of Congress Cataloging in Publication Data will be
found on the last printed page of this book

Publication of this book has been aided by a grant from
the Paul Mellon Fund of Princeton University Press

This book has been composed in Linotron Aldus and Palatino

Clothbound editions of Princeton University Press books
are printed on acid-free paper, and binding materials are
chosen for strength and durability

Printed in the United States of America by Princeton
University Press, Princeton, New Jersey

Designed by Laury A. Egan

FOR JOHN

CONTENTS

vii

ACKNOWLEDGMENTS

Some of the poems in this collection were first published in the following magazines: "In Order to Perceive" in *Prairie Schooner*; "The Man Hidden Behind the Drapes," "All the Elements of the Scene," "The Literary Man," "Capturing the Scene," "What the Body Means to Belief," "Suppose Your Father Was a Redbird," "The Rites of Passage," "The Significance of Location," "By Hearing the Same Story Over and Over" in *Poetry Northwest*; "The Literary Adventure," "Portrait," "Synthesizing the Word," "A Giant Has Swallowed the Earth," "Concepts and Their Bodies (The Boy in the Field Alone)," "Achieving Perspective," "The Determinations of the Scene" in *Poetry*; "Struck Seven Times" and "Watching Dreams" in *The Southern Review*; "How to Stay Safe in the City" in *The Beloit Poetry Journal*; "Crocodile God" in *Poet and Critic*; "The Success of the Hunt" in *The Iowa Review*; "Old Women" in *Mississippi Review*; "Second-Story Ballroom" in *Zahir*; "Dwarf" in *Southern Poetry Review*; "NASA Takes a 63-Year-Old Poet to the First Space Station" and "Without Violence" in *Bellingham Review*.

"Determining Location," "The First Norther," "How the Field, Without Being Touched, Can Be Altered," "The Fear of Falling," "Being Defined," "On Your Imminent Departure: Considering the Relative Importance of Various Motions," "How the Moon Becomes Itself," "Coming of Age," and "The Brain Creates Itself" first appeared in *The Ark River Review*, were copyrighted in 1980/81, and are here reprinted by permission of the editors.

The poem, "For Stephen Drawing Birds," originally appeared in *The New Yorker*.

Some of these poems were first printed in a slightly different form.

Part I

In Order to Perceive

At first you see nothing. The experience is similar
To opening your eyes wide as white marbles
Inside the deepest cave, beneath tons of limestone,
Or being awake in a dark room, your head
Under a heavy blanket.

Then someone suggests there is a single candle
Wavering far off in one corner, flickering red.
You think you see it
As someone else draws your attention to the sharp
Beaming wing tips, the white end of the beak,
The obvious three points of the wild goose overhead
And the seven-starred poinsettia to the west, the bright
Cluster at its belly.

You are able to recognize, when you are shown,
The sparks flying from the mane of the black stallion,
The lightning of his hooves as he rears,
And in the background a thick forest spreading
To the east, each leaf a distinct pinprick of light.

Then you begin to notice things for yourself,
A line of torches curving along a black valley,
A sparkling flower, no bigger than a snowflake,
Shining by itself in the northwest coordinate.
It is you who discovers the particular flash
Of each tooth inside the bear's open mouth and the miners
With their lighted helmets rising in a row.

How clear and explicit, you tell someone with confidence,
That ship, each separate gleaming line of its rigging,
The glowing dots of the oars, the radiating
Eyes of the figure on the prow, the corners
Of each sail lit.

Soon there is no hesitation to the breadth
Of your discoveries. Until one night during the long
Intensity of your observation, you look so perfectly
That you finally see yourself, off in the distance
Among the glittering hounds and hunters, beside the white
Shadows of the swans. There are points of fire
At your fingertips, a brilliance at the junctures
Of your bones. You watch yourself floating,
Your heels in their orbits, your hair spreading
Like a phosphorescent cloud, as you rise slowly,
A skeleton of glass beads, above the black desert,
Over the lanterned hillsides and on out through the hollow
Stretching directly overhead.

CONTAINMENT

Across the surface of the egg, couched
In the marsh weeds, a fragile
Break appears, releasing
Light for the first time.

Hung in the top of the still sycamore,
The cradle has no name
Until the wind and the sky against which it functions
Allow it to become itself.

The moon, completely full
And self-contained, is held in its place
By the black circular muscle of the night
And by that power alone.

Cracked from its base
To the break at the top of its head,
The cradle no longer depends
On the containment of the sky.
The egg, by holding night tightly
In one place long enough, has allowed
It to assume a different name.
Strung up in the sycamore, the moon
Is completely broken, the pieces
Of its shell having spilled its shadow
For the first time.

DWARF

There is a dwarf in my ancestry.
He gleams from behind my grandmother's stories,
Peeping through the shadowy legs of a grandfather's uncle.
Crouching beside potted palms in the parlor,
Eyes gauging above fanned fronds,
He is a toadish coquette.
He stares,
A lizard who has seen us first,
Steadily.
A statue with eyes assaying,
His vertical pupils shine against grey stone.

Abashed adult with no stature,
He hurries with a twisted gait,
Clicking on nights when love is quiet,
Popping up, a clown out of a coffin,
Putting hesitancy in the laughing chatter
Of maternal blood,
Poking his tilted head around the lattices
Of prospective marriages.
He giggles within the blurred faces
Of my unborn children,
In the restive fears of my own beginning.

He is
The one thing common to all my aunts.

OLD WOMEN

I live with old women,
Grandaunts, maternal great cousins,
Aged mothers of my mother.
They crowd to my house,
Still in their skirts,
Spectacled and black creped,
Mumbling to their hands.
Their white hair is as thin and dry as desert grass.
The loose skin on their upper arms
Hangs like a pale silk purse.
Their milk-blue eyes were once brown.

Sitting with me at dinner,
Wizened old leather sticks,
They eat with deliberation,
Jutting their lower lips to catch their spoons,
Dripping tea on their bosoms.
They study the tilt of a fork,
The glint of the butter on peas.

Always before me, moving down hallways,
They inch out of doorways into my path,
Shuffling with legs bent like weak candles,
So slow the room at the end is a strange city.
There is no way around.

In our chairs at night,
I watch them nodding, snoring the gurgle of the old,
Jaws open on their chests.
They jerk awake and wonder who I am.

One by one they bring their deaths—
The spasms and failures,
The slow drowning of lying prone,
The plug of phlegm corked in the throat,
The string pulled too tightly

7

Down the left side of the cranium,
Drawing the wrist, wedding band and all,
To the chest permanently.

My hands are on their elbows.
I have watched all their steps.

SECOND-STORY BALLROOM

Think how the soldiers took down every mirror
In the second-story ballroom, how they left
The bare walls standing as if they had their hands
Between their knees. Think how they carried
Those plates of glass down the stairs,
The heavy gilt frames holding candles
In gold roses half-opened. They took them
To the forest behind the house,
Propped them against the trees and began
Their target practice. Every shot hitting
Right between the eyes meant the forehead cracked
Open perfectly with a blinding light, fell apart
In slivers of silver jangling like bells
Against the earth.

Think then of all the dancers dancing
Past the darkened windows of the second-story ballroom.
Picture their dusty satins, their shadowy brocades.
Listen to the hush and swish of their movements
Down the length of the hall,
Across the blank corridors, round
And round back again.

The Reincarnated

Before our common ancestor knew itself,
It was many things. For one millennium it washed
Back and forth on the bottom of the sea. The bowling
Of the surf, it rolled lathers of sand ahead of it
And caught the green jelly of tiny creatures in its girth.
It sang salt and never kept its brow dry.

Between the time of redwoods and the peaks
Of the Kofa Range, it was mist on the desert.
It clung to the backs of beetles swung to windward
Of the dunes. It dipped down stems of dead weeds
To mouse pits and snake caverns, to live roots waiting.
It drifted in drops and became moisture seeping
To every crack in the sand.

Before our ancestor recognized itself, it was the quiet
Of the gorge rising slowly in pale blue smoke.
It surrounded and shaped itself to everything
It passed—leaf fungus, butt of rock, fur jackal.
Inside of us today is a hollow space left
For the wide bird holding in white above the firs.

Our ancestor has been polar ice and the camel's nostril,
The dorsal fin of transparent fish. Like the flying fox
And the porpoise, it has moved in darkness by sound alone.
It has lived in mold underground with every one of its fingers
Cut off. It has come back each time, adding to itself,
Recalling everything it has been before.

Shatter of primal moss, remnant of lizard hair, clay
Hooves and extinct thumbprints;
Reader, try hard to remember.

10

Suppose Your Father Was a Redbird

Suppose his body was the meticulous layering
Of graduated down which you studied early,
Rows of feathers increasing in size to the hard-splayed
Wine-gloss tips of his outer edges.

Suppose, before you could speak, you watched
The slow spread of his wing over and over,
The appearance of that invisible appendage,
The unfolding transformation of his body to the airborne.
And you followed his departure again and again,
Learning to distinguish the red microbe of his being
Far into the line of the horizon.

Then today you might be the only one able to see
The breast of a single red bloom
Five miles away across an open field.
The modification of your eye might have enabled you
To spot a red moth hanging on an oak branch
In the exact center of the Aurorean Forest.
And you could define for us, "hearing red in the air,"
As you predict the day pollen from the poppy
Will blow in from the valley.

Naturally you would picture your faith arranged
In filamented principles moving from pink
To crimson at the final quill. And the red tremble
Of your dream you might explain as the shimmer
Of his back lost over the sea at dawn.
Your sudden visions you might interpret as the uncreasing
Of heaven, the bones of the sky spread,
The conceptualized wing of the mind untangling.

Imagine the intensity of your revelation
The night the entire body of a star turns red
And you watch it as it rushes in flames
Across the black, down into the hills.

11

If your father was a redbird,
Then you would be obligated to try to understand
What it is you recognize in the sun
As you study it again this evening
Pulling itself and the sky in dark red
Over the edge of the earth.

WITHOUT VIOLENCE

That cat who comes during sleep, quiet
On his cushioned claws, without violence,
Who enters the house with a low warm rattle
In his throat; that cat who has been said
To crawl into a baby's crib without brushing
The bars, to knit his paws on the pale
Flannel of the infant's nightdress, to settle
In sleep chin to chin with the dear one
And softly steal the child's breath
Without malice, as easily as pulling
A silk scarf completely through a gold ring;

The same cat who has been known to nudge
Through castle doors, to part tent flaps,
To creep to the breasts of brave men,
Ease between their blankets, to stretch
Full length on the satin bodices of lovely
Women, to nuzzle their cheeks with his great
Feline mane; it was that cat who leaped last night
Through the west window of father's bedroom,
Who chose to knead his night's rest on my father's
Shoulder, who slept well, breathing deeply,
Leaving just before dawn to saunter toward
The north, his magnificent tail and rump
Swaying with a listless and gorgeous grace.

Coming of Age

It begins with the bones.
They must be light, delicate
As tea leaves, intricate as white wires
Glowing like glass threads,
A structure of thin hollow shells showing
The moon on full nights with no shadow.

Barely covered with pale silver skin,
They must extend from the shoulder blades
To points far beyond the furthest extension
Of the middle finger stretched outward. Tipping
And angular, free of movement,
They will develop muscles in time.

Remaining weightless as frost,
Unfractured, they must be covered completely
With silk sorrels and strings, as easy to the breeze
As tassles on a willow, fine as cobweb,
Layered like the first fronds
Of the lattice fern uncurling.

Almost invisible then, one night, without sound,
Without touching anyone, they will remember
How to rise, how to open wide like two tall gates
Swinging apart, how to lift up, taking into themselves
More hollow stars, more thick knots of space
Than they can ever encompass.

FOR STEPHEN DRAWING BIRDS

They catch your eye early, those rising black
Out of the water oaks at dusk or those skimming
The grey lakes at dawn. You know you must learn
Them by name, calling the redstart, pointing out
The towhee, the slate-colored junco. You begin
To trace their drummings through the forest, the click
Of their matings in the rocks and grow accustomed
To waiting, sketchbook in hand, for the mottled
Vireo to nurse at the fruit tree, the woodcock to rise
To the spring willow bait. You are patient
With the snow goose appearing at the bottom of the reeds
And the thrasher untangling itself from the hedgerow.
What luck, the day you find a whole cliff of gannets,
Their pale yellow heads as smooth as eggs, their eyelids
And nostrils distinctly blue.

Matching pencil to feather, you begin to take them
One by one—the marbled owl pulling at the skull
Of the lemming, the dusky tanager in the afternoon
Snipping at dragonflies. How well you execute
Their postures, the wings of the overland dove spread
Like a Japanese fan, the jackdaw frozen
At the moment of his descent into the locust.

It grows easier and easier. Soon the cedar shrike stops
On his own and waits for you, gripped to the fence post.
The grosbeak rests all day on the limb by your page,
And when you picture the rare azure-throated swallow,
He suddenly materializes under the eaves, preparing
His mudball. In the evening before the fire,
As you remember the Réunion solitaire, the giant auk,
They appear in the room, roosting on the ginger jars
Above the mantelpiece. You even wake one morning
To discover that the lark bunting has been nesting
Under your knuckles just as you dreamed he was.
There is a definite stir of preening among your papers.

15

Tonight, a strange chukal hen has flown to the cornice
Above your window. The invisible grey-green thimble bird
Is slowly coming into sight by your glass, and perched
On the bedpost, an unmarked polar hawk is watching
With his stern golden eye over the entire length of your quilt.

STRUCK SEVEN TIMES

He knows them all—ball lightning twice,
One dancing a full minute over his desk;
Two years later, the forked straddling the lawn
From his shoulder to the gate. In August of '65
The beaded bounced across the field like a stone
Over water, right into the window from which he watched.
Knocked out for three days, he was blind
For a month. He has been gripped since by the ribbon,
The streaked, the relative of St. Elmo's fire.

He grows weak now at the sight of melted lead, ill
At the odor of singed meat. He can't remember
The meaning of "accident." Jesus, in the morning
He believes in the finger of God, at night
In the rapier of Baal. He retraces his thoughts
Prior to each encounter, looking for clues. He studies
The similarities of sins current at the time,
The direction of his feet, the inclination of his head.
Who knows what might be attracted by the power
Of certain wishes?

Working nightly, he discovers that the sum of the dates
Of his confrontations equals his age times
The possible year of his death. Gradually he develops
An affinity for weather balloons. He blesses cats.
Lightning rods become a fetish, the spiraled,
The spiked, the pre-Civil War. He begins to fantasize
On the evolution of their designs.

He learns to make friends with electro-physicists,
Drawn to the terminology of ampere upheaval, stroke
Currents. He wills his body to the Franklin Institute
For the Study of Magnetic Disturbances in Human Form,
Becomes convinced that the chemical make-up of his blood
Is the inverse replica of cumulous vapor. He almost soars
Being bound in the rhetoric of blinding discharges,
The shock of flashing impacts recalled.

Even his dreams are totally dominated by Kansas,
Thunderheads, the third-story turret of an isolated farm.

It's his own fault now. His entire future
Depends on the eighth.

WATCHING DREAMS

From the case notes of Adelaide Monroe,
author of *The Intrigues of the Unconscious*.

What happens when you begin your journal,
Keeping it on the table by the bed, each dream
Immediately transferred to the page?
The dream-mind, aware of being studied, never forgets
The pencil and pad in the shadow to the far left.
Pleased at its reception, for instance, it might be encouraged
To repeat the mastiff of last week, enlarging
Its feet, chaining it for diversion to the cellar door.
And the frogs lining the road you walked in your dream
Last night must be embellished by the scrutiny
They receive this morning.

Suppose a dream, causing its own termination,
Wakes you at 3:12 A.M., and you record the room
In which you were anxiously selecting clothing
With your mother. You describe the nature and color
Of the garments, the depth of the closet, but forget
To mention the sense of thunder outside,
Which was crucial. This faulty account must influence
Subsequent dreams.

Assured of an attentive audience, the dream
Might be tempted to play tricks, might be capable
Of wit. Suppose the dream is subtle enough
To portray itself being watched. The dream becomes
The flower in the dream, alone in a mowed field
Meticulously fondled. The dream becomes the dead father
In the dream to whom one looks for signs.
Suppose the dream, aware of the hidden observer, learns
To say what it knows the dreamer wishes to hear—

19

"This is God speaking." The conscious mind
Can claim innocence.

Watching the journal with its one eye,
The dream knows its own inventiveness
And never forgets who it is it entertains.

The Caretakers

They prepare the way for morning. Naked
And completely grey, they sweep
The walks using brooms without bristles.
For them alone, all the dust of the desert
Lies down in one silk face flat beneath the moon.

They carry eggs like candles cupped in their hands
From one nest to another. They untangle the fur
Of the willow, straighten the necks of flowers,
Suck the honey of their stamens, the horns
Of their groins upward. How their tongues
Influence the funnels of leaves.

Searching among jack mice and tree tarsiers, fish
And marmosets, they pinch shut the eyes
Of those who have died without warning and pull
Shadows to cover the clearing where the sexton beetle
Works. They thrum on hollow trunks as if their fingers
Had no joints.

Watching over the bodies of those sleeping
Like stones in a field, they tuck at their toes,
Measure their breathing with their own glass eyes,
Push the cold bowl of pain under the bed.

They are the ones who whisper over metal accidents
Refined definitions of failure.

Near the end, their arms begin to stretch
Twice as long as their bodies upward. Their faces lengthen
With the twist of peeled cypress until the cups
Of their cheekbones glow and their mouths become split
Ovals among the trees disappearing without a sound
Into the overall sky exactly their color.

THE RITES OF PASSAGE

The inner cell of each frog egg laid today
In these still open waters is surrounded
By melanin pigment, by a jelly capsule
Acting as cushion to the falling of the surf,
As buffer to the loud crow-calling
Coming from the cleared forests to the north.

At 77° the single cell cleaves in 90 minutes,
Then cleaves again and in five hours forms the hollow
Ball of the blastula. In the dark, 18 hours later,
Even as a shuffle in the grass moves the shadows
On the shore and the stripes of the moon on the sand
Disappear and the sounds of the heron jerk
Across the lake, the growing blastula turns itself
Inside out unassisted and becomes a gut.

What is the source of the tension instigating next
The rudimentary tail and gills, the cobweb of veins?
What is the impetus slowly directing the hard-core
Current right up the scale to that one definite moment
When a fold of cells quivers suddenly for the first time
And someone says loudly "heart," born, beating steadily,
Bearing now in the white water of the moon
The instantaneous distinction of being liable to death?

Above me, the full moon, round and floating deep
In its capsule of sky, never trembles.
In ten thousand years it will never involute
Its white frozen blastula to form a gut,
Will never by a heart be called born.

Think of that part of me wishing tonight to remember
The split-second edge before the beginning,
To remember by a sudden white involution of sight,
By a vision of tension folding itself
Inside clear open waters, by imitating a manipulation
Of cells in a moment of distinction, wishing to remember
The entire language made during that crossing.

PART II

How to Stay Safe in the City

It is best to make this rule:
Keep your door of hard hickory barred,
No exceptions.

If you should hear the bell sound twice,
Go to the keyhole and listen. Heavy breathing
Means two or more people taller than you
Are waiting. Stay quiet.

If the knocker sounds, it is the pretentious
Lady in purple, wanting your skin color, the amount
Of change in your pockets.
Ignore her.

Anyone who calls through your lock announcing
His mission too loudly is a person
In robes, clearly fictitious. If you come face to face
With him, you will be accosted.
Don't answer.

Be careful, careful. A loud insistent
Rapping with bare knuckles means someone needs
Assistance badly. He will be ugly, humpbacked
And reeking. If you allow it, he will fall
On your neck and remain there.
Leave the door shut.

Let no one on the other side see your face.
Peer from behind curtains, through BB-sized slots,
Cracks by the casement. Gauge your callers
With mirrors and shadows but stay hidden.
This is to your advantage.

Beware of dwarves and pygmies, monks,
Spacemen, young girls with flowers and candles,
Animals that come alone.

On windy nights push a chair against the knob.
The clawing and scratching, the whispering
Of the hinges, the shifting of the door
On its axis are the sounds of those
Who have been fed without milk, bearing you no kinship.
They bring with them their boney cats, bare branches,
Birds without feet. Stay alert, they will be there
Until morning.

After a sudden heavy knocking
Should you hear nothing but the shuffle of boots,
The clanking of tools, quickly turn off every light
In the house. Start backing down your hallway
As quietly as you can toward that secret door
In the corner under your bed,
At which you must begin to tap
Softly, softly.

How You Came

It's a wonder how you came
Clear across a city,
Jumping the roofs of marble towers
Like stepping stones,
Weaving under metal girders,
Tripping up orange steel,
Bolts as big as sausages.

Like a bully goat over bridges,
Ignoring dark trolls and their gleaming spikes,
You were brave,
In the black beneath concrete viaducts,
Their undersides pinned with the brushwork of birds
And dripping the green of last week's water.

Past a thousand, thousand wooden doors,
You circled the rooms of glass buildings,
Skirted cement walls,
Walking sideways just above rivers.

You balanced like dusk,
Even moss couldn't cause a stumble.

Without pebbles or string,
Without magnets or stars,
Without even my line
Blue on white paper,
You came,
Found your way at last,
Turning, like a branch bent quick in the wind,
The latch at my very window.

The Question of Affection

We don't know yet what it means to be touched,
To be the recipient of caresses, what the ear
Learns of itself when its lines are followed
By the finger of somebody else.

We know the spine of the infant can expand,
The neck grow sturdy, the shoulder blades facile
By fondling alone. The acuity of the eye is increased,
The lung capacity doubled by random nuzzles
To the ribs.

But we don't understand what the mind perceives
When the thigh's length is fixed by the dawdling
Of the lover's hand, when the girth of the waist
Is defined by the arms of a child.

An affectionate ear on the belly must alter
The conception of the earth pressing itself against the sky.
An elbow bent across the chest must anticipate
Early light angled over the lake. The curl of the pea
Can be understood as one hand caught carefully inside another.

Cores and cylinders, warm boundaries and disappearing curves,
What is it we realize when these interruptions of space
Are identified with love in the touch of somebody else?

I must remember now what it was I recognized
In the sky outside the window last night
As I felt the line of my shoulder drawn
In the trace of your lips.

BEING DEFINED

This room and the wind outside
Create the facts of each other tonight—
The wind identified by the interferences
Of the eaves, the walls known
By what they separate.

This light, dim beneath its brass shade,
Is repeated in the curve of your glass,
Defined again in your eyes, becomes
The ghost of itself on the rise of your cheek.
You give the light these places to exist.

And by the line of your neck, my finger
Becomes an aspect of caress.
By the boundaries of your forehead, my hand
Becomes a trace of gentleness.

What I am now
Is only she who binds spaces for you.
And your breath, the softest motion
Against my ear, will never understand itself
In any other terms.

SEDUCED BY EAR ALONE

Someone should explain how it happens, starting
With the dull stimulation of anvil and stirrups,
The established frequency of shifting air molecules
Initiated by your voice, entering my ear.
The mind, having learned how, can find the single silk
Strand of your breath anywhere, latch on and remember.

But not actually touching the body at all,
How do words alone ease the strictures of the palms,
Alter the tendency of the thighs, cause
The eyes to experience visions? I can see clearly
The stark white sliver of passion running a mile deep
In your whisper.

Maybe the ease of your voice suggests
The bliss of some previous state—sleeping
In a deep crevice at the top of a mountain, the eyes
Sealed tight, or being fed by motion in warm water
At the edge of the sea. By the twist of leaves
In a forest of poplars, I understand how light is fractioned
And born again in the aspects of your words.
I listen like an eddy in deep water turning easily
From one existence to another. I want now
To be covered by you.

And alone on any night, if the wind in the trees
Should sound by accident like the timbre of your voice,
I can be fooled for an instant, feeling suddenly in the dark
Estimable and saved.

HEARING THE UNEXPECTED

Hearing is not an instinct. Deaf children, cured,
Must be taught to hear. Beginning with the smallest
Silver bell, the brain is instructed on the isolation
Of ringing, the counter clunk of the wooden block.
The mind must be led to single out and name the rush
Of wild ducks slapping across the lake, wind rubbing
Backward on the trees, the teacher's voice
Saying, "These are your hands clapping."

The tremble of the inner ear is constant. The selection
By the brain is taught. "That is the mucous slide
Of the worm through sand. Those are spindle shells
Knocking in the surf."

What becomes then of sounds that enter
The ear without names—the whine
Of the moon muffled in clouds, the high-pitched
Terror of the earth turning into night?
This evening, the hissing and sizzling
Of the inflexible social vectors bound to this group
Have been completely missed.

We must practice fine distinctions.
"Hear the sloving of evening's soft sheet
Over the hills. Hear the hard ranchet
Of the wish abandoned. That is the sking
Of the roof's edge against the sky."

Listen. Listen. This is crucial.
In time the ear may even be capable of hearing
Its own function.

THE FIRST NORTHER

1.

Arriving all evening, turning up the bellies
Of oak leaves, parting the edges
Of cotton hulls and spikelet shafts, it comes,
Having swept first over deserts
Of black tundra, having brushed the flanks
Of the musk ox, descended into the dark
Bubbles of the pipits' lungs and out again.
It has been slack in the wings
Of the snowy owl, static in the webs
Of a thousand firs, but it comes now
Pressing particles of down
And whale smoke, penetrating windows
With spirits of cedar, frost
From the lemming's mouth.

2.

Aware of its presence, what will happen to us then
If we choose to leave this room together,
If we walk out among the trees maintaining
Their broken intentions against the wind
And stop beside the wall, feeling the hiss
Of Arctic lichen in our sweaters, the rush
Of frozen grasses in our hands?
You and I, tasting the same air that touched
The eye of the caribou in migration,
Taking into our lungs the same molecules
That reckoned their motion over icy plains
By darkness alone? Surrounded
And utterly possessed, how will you speak
To me then? How will I ever reply?

Achieving Perspective

Straight up away from this road,
Away from the fitted particles of frost
Coating the hull of each chick pea,
And the stiff archer bug making its way
In the morning dark, toe hair by toe hair,
Up the stem of the trillium,
Straight up through the sky above this road right now,
The galaxies of the Cygnus A cluster
Are colliding with each other in a massive swarm
Of interpenetrating and exploding catastrophes.
I try to remember that.

And even in the gold and purple pretense
Of evening, I make myself remember
That it would take 40,000 years full of gathering
Into leaf and dropping, full of pulp splitting
And the hard wrinkling of seed, of the rising up
Of wood fibers and the disintegration of forests,
Of this lake disappearing completely in the bodies
Of toad slush and duckweed rock,
40,000 years and the fastest thing we own,
To reach the one star nearest to us.

And when you speak to me like this,
I try to remember that the wood and cement walls
Of this room are being swept away now
Molecule by molecule, in a slow and steady wind,
And nothing at all separates our bodies
From the vast emptiness expanding, and I know
We are sitting in our chairs
Discoursing in the middle of the blackness of space.
And when you look at me

I try to recall that at this moment
Somewhere millions of miles beyond the dimness
Of the sun, the comet Biela, speeding
In its rocks and ices, is just beginning to enter
The widest arc of its elliptical turn.

ON YOUR IMMINENT DEPARTURE: CONSIDERING THE RELATIVE IMPORTANCE OF VARIOUS MOTIONS

Which is more important, the motion of the wind
Forcing every top-heavy reed along the shore
To precisely the same height, or the manipulations
Of the moon moving the white lines of our window slowly
Across the wall of this room?

Or your hand in motion across my back, suggesting
The scarcely noticeable rising of the lake,
The possible empty sky deepening without interruption
In this bed moving relative to the moon
Twenty-five miles away from two minutes ago?

Consider the various subtleties becoming singular
In the eleven motions of our bodies
Pinpointed together here on the night-facing side
Of the earth tilted in summer angle toward the sun
Consistently dragged by the galaxy further out
Into no known direction whatever.

The mind is the only object
That can ever return to this same spot exactly
Over and over.

Beside the calm of the pine trees brushing
Against each other in the dark, how important
Is the hard twist of my refusal to believe in your departure,
You going away alone, westward at one speed
Over forests moving eastward at another, above clouds
Creating southward-flowing shadows touching
Everything left below? Inside this room, how irreversible
Is the steady speed of the inevitable, keeping up,
Always keeping up with us?

Picture the motion of my voice rising now
To ask you this question, leaving itself forever afterward
Motionless in mid-air?

TRYING MAGIC

Do you think if I looked at him hard and said
Over and over to the back of his head, "Don't be hurt,"
It would make a difference? Some people believe
In chants, the effects of memorable sound repeated.
They speak of a resonating power building inward
Under the breastbone, pressing outward simultaneously,
Gathering momentum in the form of circles radiating
Until they reach something somewhere that can make a difference.

Knowing that lead remains in ashes, I could write
In pencil, "Remember how definitely his attitude
Can be injured. Just remember that." And I could burn
The message in the light of the last sun of the equinox,
Leave the ashes in a jar at a spot designated
For those having influence.

Suppose I present him to the sky.
Suppose for three nights in a row I think of him
Spread naked against the stars. And I follow
Every line of his body with my eyes, from one foot
Up the thigh, the striations of the belly,
Throat, head, down the other side, filling in
The triangle of the groin, over and over
Thinking, "Shielded, shielded." Would it make a difference,
Like immersing him in a beneficent river,
Every pore protected?

I can believe in the energy of wishing.
How the body must engender electricity for the speech,
The chemistry of concentration in the pitch of the voice.
I could make someone notice if I sent this with great force
Sparkling into the atmosphere on a windless night—
"I *wish* him not to be hurt again."

Then shouldn't some bold angel somewhere hear
And help us?

39

HIRING THE MAN WHO BUILDS FIRES FOR A LIVING

He comes when I ask him, during the last half hour
Of evening, begins with his earthen circles,
His rings of rock. Infuriating swagger,
He carries about him the distinct odor of mitigating humus.

But he knows his business. He disappears again and again
Into the trees, taken as if the forest knew him personally,
And comes back always from another direction, his arms
Full of branches having fallen themselves
From great heights without wings nights ago.

When the trees are not totally black, not yet fully entrenched
In the grey sky, imagine how he kneels down
And bends close, how he proceeds with the arrangement.
What is it he believes about this altar? He lays
Each stick religiously as if it had grown
Toward this place from the beginning. What is he whispering
To those dried-up leaves as if they had souls?
There's a blessing here he definitely finds amusing.

I can never see at this point what it is he moves
With his hands or how he concentrates on molding
The invisible as if he could manipulate prophecy, shape
The promise to fit the gift to come. Perfect sculptor,
He knows his element thoroughly.

Watching the deep blue curtains as they fall constantly now
Among the dark trees, I admit
He knows with his breath how to make flame live.

And in the midst of it all, what can I think of a man
Who has created in this black forest tonight
A popping circus of blue-gold brilliance plummeting
With such acrobatic radiance that I laugh out loud myself?
Well, I hired him on faith. He was obliged to be
More than I expected.

40

CROCODILE GOD

Sand-warm, his toes,
His bronze calves swell like the bellies
Of round golden fish.
Movements under his skin are flashing little fins,
The ripples of silk tails.
He is oiled for beauty.

From two fingers he dangles trinkets,
A ringed cross snapped from dark river silt
On a bright morning, his two-footed cane
Dredged from the bodies of snails and eels.
He has rooted the bottoms of unknown swamps.

Sandalless,
He may swagger in his grand bodice,
Displaying mosaic wrist bands, biceps bracelets.
His sash relaxes navel high on his slender hips.
The plated collar around his throat is more than a napkin.

But it is his head,
Green as moss, bumpy as bark,
And the corners of his smile, the scaley cheeks;
It is the tilt of his long toad-spotted snout,
The exposure of numerous teeth in his cold pink smirk,
The slit-eyes (he never wonders)
And the hiss of his breath,
Smelling of salt clams, old backbones,
That cause us to
Love him.

THE VIEWPOINT OF THE UNBELIEVABLE

Suppose I believe this couch is a boat
And I am stretched out asleep at sea.
Suppose I believe I hear in this room the current
Sucking at the sides, and I feel through the tremor
Of the boat the grebe and his soft sudden
Tricking of the waves, the slip of the silver
He lifts up dripping into the sun.

Suppose I believe I am buoyant three miles above
Giant tubular worms shifting in their warm-water
Beds below. And I accept everything that hangs
Suspended beneath me—the long translucent curtains
Of jelly fish strings, the coil of the eel turning
In mid-water, in every direction the claws of crabs
Askew in the coral, and, passing in my shadow,
The furled silk of the manta ray.

And through my eyelids I can see the amoeba
Of the sun stretching in the reflection of the sea,
Like an explosion, the green neon streak of the gull shrieking.
In gusts of grey, I recognize the occasional brush stroke
Of the wind. Suppose, even beside this wall,
I believe in the continuous deep dart and stream
Of the turned fin gliding below, the glazed
Golden eye disappearing downward.

Then, if you should call to me from the other room,
And I should rise, step off without hesitation, I know
Someone watching from the shore a long way off
Will bear witness to how I moved from the boat without fear
And walked on waves.

How the Moon Becomes Itself

Think how it is altered
By what I hold in my hands when I see it.
Fingering the sharp spikes
Of a sweet-gum ball, it becomes covered
With glass thorns and glows with enmity.
Or pressing a leaf between my palms,
A sudden network of grey veins traces
Across its mountains, and it hangs
Thin and tenuous against the sky.

If I touch the fuzz of the billie's
Cocoon, it goes unfocused with fur.
The moon is so totally dependent.
With one finger, the pocks
Of the orange rind become its craters.
A white fruit, how simple to consume
It by mouth, to chew it
And spit silver seeds.

In gloves, I call it the diviner of snow,
The seer of ice. Last December,
As I stood at the door watching you leave,
It was that hard knob that will never turn.

Gripping the sides of the boat tonight
It is the essential illumination
In the throats of all fish, the way
By which water flames. And as I lie
On the hillside, my hands flat to the sheet,
It is only a cushion against which I see myself spread.

Holding your face between my hands then,
The moon appearing on your right,
As you bend to my neck, the moon
Shifting to your left, it is that coin
Definitely shining lucky side up.

PART III

ILLUMINATION

Having blown out the only candle
In the unlit room, we still thought
We could see through the dark a string
Of smoke rising from the snuffed wick.

The raccoon, fascinated by reflection,
Is unable to light his den
With his gathered bits of metal,
His scraps of foiled glass.

Standing under the yellow poplar at noon,
She cares nothing for the tree,
Being interested only in the way light
Moves across its turning leaves.

If we study a mirror in a black cave
Long enough, the absence of light
Will be made clearly visible.
Sitting on a high branch in the cloudy night,
Can the raccoon see what expectations
Light has led him to understand?
When the last leaf of the yellow poplar
Has been blown away,
Will the eye of the girl remembering
Be the only body left there for light?

THE BRAIN CREATES ITSELF

A thread of tissues takes shape
As I first comprehend the red rock crossed twice
By the fringe-toed lizard at dusk.
A unique chain of cells becomes actual
As I identify the man beneath the white beech
And his influence on the nesting kiwi bird.

A new vein of reactions must arise
With my discovery of the dark star
On the rim of Sirius. A split-second network
Must be brought into being as I find the African
Dung beetle's egg buried in the elephant bolus.
And for each unacknowledged aspect of the purple
Spikenard beside the marsh-elder-to-be, for each unrecognized
Function of the ogre-faced stick spider at dawn,
A potential neuron is absent in the frontal lobe.

Imagine the molecular structure I create
As I contemplate the galapagos dragon
At the bottom of the ocean stopping his heart
At will, dying for three minutes motionless
In the suck and draw of the sea. Imagine,
When I study his rapid zig-zag swagger to the surface,
How a permanent line like silver makes its way
From the inner base of my skull to the top of my head.

And as I look at your face, following the contours
From your forehead to your chin, coming back again
To your eyes, I can almost picture the wide cranial
Web developing as my definite affection
For these particulars.

How the Body in Motion Affects the Mind

Consider the mind
As it perceives the hands rising
To grasp the tree branch, each finger
Tightening on the limb and the effort
Of the arms pulling the body upward.
What pattern of interpretation synthesized
From that event
Must establish itself in the neocortex?

We know there are precise configurations
Forced on the brain by the phenomena
Of the hand clenched, by the tucking in
Of the thumb, by the sight of the foot
Flexed on the ground and pushing backward.
How do these configurations influence the study
Of duty or manipulate the definition
Of power? The mind, initiating the motion,
Must be altered itself
By the concepts contained in the accomplishment.

I could almost diagram on this paper
The structure of interactions implanted
In the neuronic fibers by the runner's
Leap across the dry gully. Who can say for certain
That structure has nothing to do
With the control of grief?
Think how the mind has no choice
But to accomodate itself to the restrained
Pressure of the fingertips tracing
The lover's spine. The subtlety
Of that motion must turn back
To modify the source of itself.

We are bound by the theorum of sockets and joints,
Totally united with contraction and release.
The idea of truth cannot be separated

From the action of the hand releasing
The stone at the precise apogee of the arm's motion
Or from the spine's flexibility easing
Through a wooden fence. The notion
Of the vast will not ignore the arm swinging
In motion from the shoulder or the fingers
Clasped together in alternation.

And when the infant, for the first time,
Turns his body over completely, think
What an enormous revelation in the brain
Must be forced, at that moment, to right itself.

THE MAN HIDDEN BEHIND THE DRAPES

When I entered the room and turned on the lights,
There were his feet bare beneath the edge
Of the draperies, his tendons flexed, the bony
Diamonds of his ankles shadowed. If I'd seen
His face I might have laughed.

Remember the naked feet of Christ seen so often,
Washed, kissed, dried in women's hair,
Or crossed and bleeding, pinioned
Like butterfly wings?

When I opened the door,
There were his feet below the drapes, as quiet
As if they lounged beneath a fine robe. Headlights
Moving slowly up the drive at this point
Would have fully exposed his nude body in the window,
His buttocks tensed, his face turned toward the glare
For that moment, then disappearing again into the darkness.

An artist might have pictured snow on the lawn
And a moon and a child looking out from the house
Across the way, watching the figure behind the glass,
The white panes across his back, his hands reaching
For the parting in the curtains.

When I entered the room the light spread first
In a rectangle straight across the floor to his feet,
His toes squeezing under in a crippled kind of gripping.
Someone watching from the end of the hall behind me
Would have seen my body framed in the light of the doorway
And beyond me the wall of the drapes.

Understand the particular axis at which he stood
In the vision of each different beholder, the multiple
Coordinates of hour and position and place coinciding
With the grids of light and sound and preceding

Interpretations. Consider that indeterminable effect
Of his being on the eye of the one unaware of his existence.

There is a house three blocks away that has no man
Behind the drapes. There is a house on a high sea wall
That has two men and no window. There is a house
That does not speak this language and consequently
Tells us nothing.

Almost laughing, my hand still on the door,
I stood watching his feet, and had there been an old woman
Living in the attic, then looking down through a chink in the ceiling
She would have seen in two dimensions, the knuckles of his toes,
The top of my head.

How the Field, Without Being Touched, Can Be Altered

Think of the field that surrounds
The woman in blue walking on the path.
Notice how each hair of each grain head
Beside her comes definitely into view
Against the dark relief of her jacket,
Then fades out of focus again as she passes.
Observe the expanse of her shadow
As it falters over the wheat to her east,
Turning the stalks momentarily black, taking the sun
Completely out of itself down to the earth.

Understand how the field changes.
Consider the crippled man and the aspects
Of his interactions, how his resolute
Preoccupation with stones and rain-ruts
Creates a new and distinct fear
Out of the terrain. A locust knocking
Against his arm produces an awkwardness
Right there among the weeds
Where it didn't exist before.

And the birds, rising now
From the hedgerow, make eight black
Changes of motion over the grasses.
How do their cries alter the concept
Of the dust pillars teetering on the pistils
Of the coneflowers? The house on the far side
Of the field, seen only when the wheat bends,
Provides justification for pronouncing the field,
On a windless day, obstructive.

Take note of how anonymity can come and go
In this field. The color of the burnished
Acres and the split tassle on the near stalks
Will not be named by the boor passing through.

53

The mouse cave will receive no identity,
And the seed of the moth
Will not be announced by the wicked.
But the fastidious will remember
The spittle bug and its location.

And we, being nowhere near the field now,
Alter it also by endowing it with the faith
Which enables us to believe, after all,
In its existence.

THE ZOO: HOW THE CAPTURED ANIMAL MAINTAINS HIS POWER

Notice how the elephant house
Accomodates its creature,
The inner wall built to withstand
The leaning of the great bulk, the post
Buried deep to survive the rub
Of the haunch. The elephant establishes
His place by demanding that the force
Of each foot
Be of prime consideration.
He must be the subject of investigation,
Being the center
Around which the zoo master must function,
The reason for the zoo master's existence at all.

An animal must prevail to insure
The survival of his prison.
The round-domed ceiling of the hippo's
Building must emulate his girth,
Leaving room for the guttural
Groans of his digestion, the expansion
Of his pig river breath.
And merely by his presence, the deer
Determines the height of his wire fence,
The dimensions of its woven pattern.

Isn't the success of the zoo based
On the master's ability to assess
The character of the cheetah's paw,
The clever teeth of the wild horse,
The shoulder muscles of the brown bear
At bay? Dependent on perceiving
Ultimate lizardry, he must divine the quirks
Of the iguana, the antipathies of the anole.

Observe how each animal causes his environment
To duplicate the ancient veldt or the primitive
Rain forest, the Arctic Circle at dusk.
The essence of alligator will bring forth
The murky pool, the persistent odor
Of fish bone and water gut.

Remember, not only must the roof
Of the great ape's domain be structured to withstand
The vibrations of his screeching, but the beams
Must also be bolstered against the pressure
Of the jungle tree which will take root by itself,
Spread, push upward to fit exactly
The black fingered grip enduring there,
The long arms waiting.

CONCEPTS AND THEIR BODIES
(THE BOY IN THE FIELD Alone)

Staring at the mud turtle's eye
Long enough, he sees *concentricity* there
For the first time, as if it possessed
Pupil and iris and oracular lid,
As if it grew, forcing its own gene of circularity.
The concept is definitely
The cellular arrangement of sight.

The five amber grasses maintaining their seedheads
In the breeze against the sky
Have borne *latitude* from the beginning,
Secure *civility* like leaves in their folds.
He discovers *persistence* in the mouth
Of the caterpillar in the same way
As he discovers clear syrup
On the broken end of the dayflower,
Exactly as he comes accidently upon
The mud crown of the crawfish.

The spotted length of the bullfrog leaping
Lakeward just before the footstep
Is not bullfrog, spread and sailing,
But the body of *initiative* with white glossy belly.
Departure is the wing let loose
By the dandelion, and it does possess
A sparse down and will not be thought of,
Even years later, even in the station
At midnight among the confusing lights,
As separate from that white twist
Of filament drifting.

Nothing is sharp enough to disengage
The butterfly's path from *erraticism*.

And *freedom* is this September field
Covered this far by tree shadows
Through which this child chooses to run
Until he chooses to stop,
And it will be so hereafter.

What the Body Means to Belief

Belief in the evil of the sun, we know,
Without doubt, affects the complexion,
Causing a paling of the pigment, a fading
Of the hue. Shut away, avoiding windows,
The demeanor grows ashen. The daylight view
Of the face is thus depressed, giving good reason
For a siding with night.

And that one who is convinced of a return
By sea, who watches from the slippery cliffs
Above the bay, learns to see the ocean well,
Detecting on the furthest rim every surge
That is not wave, every rising corner
That is not brine or fin. Even on the blank side
Of the horizon, he can distinguish the approach
Of the man-made. His stance becomes gradually
Bent at an angle into the wind, easing his balance.
There is medical evidence of salt immunity
In his eyes, of a definite modification of calcium
Along the spine.

And the eyesight of the necromancer, as a result
Of his belief in the candle and its powers,
Becomes capable of isolating the split-second flutter
Of the flame. The physician notes a swelling
Of the optic buds, an increased number of cells devoted
To sporadic flashes. And having faith in bodily
Extremities, the nerves at his outer perimeters
Grow agitated with practice, clever at detecting
The slightest stir. He locates a moth merely
By feeling the disturbance of air about its wings.
In his scalp, he can count the concentration
Of electrical charge at the ends of his hair.

Will you believe that a sincere belief in the beneficent
Relaxes the muscles at the corners of the lips,

59

Precipitates a minute lapse in the strictures
Of the rib cage? That this allows for an expansion
Of the capillaries enabling them to carry
More oxygen to the frontal lobe, thus greatly increasing
The capacity for love, causing the chin
To tilt upward, the hands to turn naturally out?

Understand that a total belief in this poem
Will cause a subtle squint of perception
In the left eyelid, a permanent twist
In the analytic gyrus of the outer brain.

An Act of Conviction

From the case notes of Dr. Charles Atlon,
Resident Drama Psychiatrist, Liverpool School of the Dramatic Arts.

That person who makes a deliberate decision to pretend
Madness, to act out the part with conviction,
In time becomes insane. Such is the global influence
Of the brain on itself. The pronunciation of each word
Is not without its effects, as he studies his role, learning
What is to be expected of one practicing the unpredictable.

He begins his performance, leaving fragments of notes
Where they will be found easily, raving letters
Torn to make sense in pieces. He has a stroke
Of genius—to sidle across the lawn with his nose
Held high, pretending to be led by the odor
Of wing-berries over the wall. Tricks of this sort
Make him laugh. He memorizes his act like a dancer.

In time he becomes a master at the semblance
Of misinterpretation, mixing the nitwit with the pea tom,
Disturbing the boundaries of body and place. He practices
Transferring his awareness from behind his face
To the pink primrose vase on the étagère. He can't resist
Believing in the words of his own fabrications
When they are spoken out loud.

He becomes more and more proficient. In the midst
Of company, he stares out the window at a broad
Expanse of snow, contemplating the vacancies of calling
Oneself insane. He adopts the gestures of madness
So perfectly that he finds himself by habit
Curled beneath the kitchen table, considering the state
Of the sane who pretends himself mad. He resists
Every effort to break down his talents.

When the performance is over—unrestrained sanity,
Madness acquainted with itself—who can blame him?
What else can the brain know of itself
Except through its own words?

Handling Despair

The following is an account of a study made by wiring various sections of a musician's brain for monitoring by a computer with color graphics. The study was made as the musician performed with his symphony orchestra.

During the pianissimo beginning, the area of his brain
Controlling thumb and forefinger appears on the computer screen
Agitated in purple and shifting in heat. There is visible
Chemical interchange alternating in tones of brown
On the portion of the frontal lobe transferring
The printed symbol to muscular fact.

Well into the passage adagio, his brain clearly identifies
The falling mouthpiece of a trumpeter which appears
On the screen as a red flash barely encroaching
Upon the steady perception in blue of the conductor's baton
Lying in the same mode as the purple regulatory
Line of his pulse.

During the marche grande, the activity in the ivory
Parietal lobe is his sudden vision of a satin sash
Lying across his wife's lap. This vision hardly affects
His contribution to the orchestral crescendo in violet
Or the clear gold stimulation of the switch to G minor
Which occurs simultaneously with the grey ease of sweat
Clocked by the brain to materialize at this temperature
Along his brow.

The sense of taut strings under his fingertips, the recognition
Of the pressure of the wooden chair against his buttocks,
Are both located in right-angle graphics just beyond
The black-and-white checkered symbol of his wife's legs
Crossing again in silk which takes precedence
Over the electrical impulse generated by a reptile-like
Dissatisfaction below the limbic area.

It is found that the composition of his unrecalled
Memories appears as the layering of a rose coiled

In light, and a shimmer above the left ear suggests
That his brain is holding in an unknown location
The knowledge that Tchaikovsky has been dead for 87 years.

Beside the pulsing orange control of his breath,
The green streaks of his eye movements and the black
Dormancy of the unacknowledged, the mathematics of his mother
Standing at the top of the wooden steps in recollection
Emerges as he begins the staggering points
Of his pizzicato into the finale.

During the last screening, his brain appears
In the indescribable colors of itself,
Displaying the clear sense he possesses now of rising
Above the stage, over the heads of the musicians, relinquishing
His instrument, to play by mind alone.

At the conclusion, there is definite concern
As to how the validity of this study might be affected
By the musician's own perusal of the results tomorrow.

Determining Location

A man, hunched beside a wall, looks south
Through the morning haze toward a ragged field.
On the sun-side of his foot, a locust stutters
Then smooths its way to silence.

The man is thinking of a woman reading
In her study at night. He sees firelight
Moving on the walls like gold moths out of focus.
The window panes are blank
As black onyx. He knows snow
Is falling outside.

Two snipe quibble in the marsh
Behind the wall. The fire hisses.
The field grows mellifluous in the heavy sun.

The man imagines the woman shifting her legs,
Continuing to read of a walkway disappearing
Through a forest of beeches. The branches
Are soft, barely sketched in early green.
A girl is running down the walk, her red
Sweater spreading like a cape behind her.
From the top of a tree a bird rises, reflecting
In his eye a rush-filled pond
And the blue rim of sky it encircles.

In the field, the woman raises her eyes,
Scarcely hearing the tick of snow, and considers
The pond whose only place is the eye of the bird.
How important are the coordinates of the winter night
In which she exists this morning?
Is it possible for the snipe to find
The beeches which are just beyond the wall?
In the study, there is only one direction

For the girl to run. The man opens his hands
To the forest whose page he has forgotten.

Heading east across the field, a truck approaches,
Carrying a small boy who believes
The side mirror contains grey-gowned figures
That rise and fall in the billowing dust.

The Determinations of the Scene

Consider one born in the desert,
How he must see his sorrow rise
In the semblance of the yucca spreading
Its thorn-covered leaves in every direction,
Pricking clear to the ends
Of his fingers. He recognizes it
And deals with it thus. He learns to ponder
Like the reptile, in a posed quiet
Of the mind, to move on the barest
Of essentials, to solve problems
Like the twisted mesquite sustaining itself.
He puts edges to the nouns of his statements,
Copying the distinct lines of the canyon in shadow
And establishes cool niches out of the sun
In every part of his dogma. He understands
His ecstacy in terms of fluidity, high spring water
In motion through the arroyo.

That one born in the forest, growing up
With canopies, must seek to secure coverings
For all of his theories. He blesses trees
And boulders, the solid and barely altered.
He is biased in terms of stable growth vertically.
And doesn't he picture his thoughts springing
From moss and decay, from the white sponge
Of fungus and porous toadstools blending?
He is shaped by the fecund and the damp,
His fertile identifications with humus
And the aroma of rain on the deepening
Forest floor. Seeing the sky only in pieces
Of light, his widest definition must be modeled
After the clearing hemmed in by trees.

And consider the child raised near the sea, impinged
Upon constantly by the surf rising in swells,
Breaking itself to permanent particles of mist

Over the cliffs. Did you really think
The constant commotion of all that fury
Would mean nothing in the formation of the vocabulary
Which he chooses to assign to God?
The surge, the explosion must constitute
The underlying dominion unacknowledged
In his approach to the cosmos.

We mustn't forget to inquire:
Against what kinds of threats must the psyche
Of the Arctic child protect itself in sleep?

BEING OF THIS STATE

In the entire night sky, in all of the inverted
Slipped-back-upon-itself almost total emptiness
With its occasional faint clusters of pinprick
Fluctuations, there is not one single
Star grateful for its own light.

And on the stalk of blossoming confusion
Outside my door, barrelheads of camelia fistfuls,
There is not one petal that esteems
The ivory ellipse of its own outer edge
Or the molecules of its own scent escaping.

Who can detect a joy of beholding in the golden
Pipe fish filtering among the golden coral
Or in the blue-bred musk ox with its shaggy frost?
Which one among the tattered fungi remembers
The favor of the damp, the gift of decay?

Along the beach the Atlantic terns rush forward
Up to their knees in salt foam and shell
Shag rolling, but not one is able to bless first
The mole crab it snips up and swallows.

Inside the network of the clearing, among the scritching
And skeetering, the thuz and the tremulous ching,
There is not one insect able to recognize the sound
Of its own beatification. Clinging to the weeds

In the middle of that broad field spread wide
And pressed against the open night, neither those insects,
Nor the hissing grasses, nor the ash-covered moon
Can ever contemplate the importance
Of the invention of praise.

SUPPOSITION

Suppose the molecular changes taking place
In the mind during the act of praise
Resulted in an emanation rising into space.
Suppose that emanation went forth
In the configuration of its occasion:
For instance, the design of rain pocks
On the lake's surface or the blue depths
Of the canyon with its horizontal cedars stunted.

Suppose praise had physical properties
And actually endured? What if the pattern
Of its disturbances rose beyond the atmosphere,
Becoming a permanent outline implanted in the cosmos—
The sound of the celebratory banjo or horn
Lodging near the third star of Orion's belt;
Or to the east of the Pleiades, an atomic
Disarrangement of the words,
"How particular, the pod-eyed hermit crab
And his prickly orange legs"?

Suppose benevolent praise,
Coming into being by our will,
Had a separate existence, its purple or azure light
Gathering in the upper reaches, affecting
The aura of morning haze over autumn fields,
Or causing a perturbation in the mode of an asteroid.
What if praise and its emanations
Were necessary catalysts to the harmonious
Expansion of the void? Suppose, for the prosperous
Welfare of the universe, there were an element
Of need involved.

How the Scene Influences Occasions

The quarrel occurring between two people standing
Under a winter oak is bound
To be regimented by the pattern of branches
Surrounding it. How can it take shape
Except inside the tangled lines
Of those black branches against the sky?
And who could think the creak and snap
Of the freezing tree would have no effect
On the choice of its syntax? The pauses forced
By the gusting wind must also render the quarrel episodic.

The mad man's curse shouted over the meadow
Rises without obstacle, expands
Over the grasses, taking in the energy
Of the unicorn beetle and the lizard worm.
It can even attach itself in its grandiosity
To the birds circling overhead.
But the same curse shouted from the cliff
Above the sea loses itself immediately,
Unrecognized and downed in mist.

Imagine how the love song sung among the roots
And bugs of high weeds is altered by the activities
Around it, as if insects burrowed in its sounds,
As if spores and vines curled through its lapses.
Think of the difference in the same song sung
On the planks of an empty shack, speared
By dusty light and rescued by a single spider.

We know how the quality of night snow
Lightens the lullaby, does not interrupt
The prayer, demures to the blessing,
How it enhances the bonfire set
Beside the frozen lake. The speech of the dullard then
Must be improved by thunder rattling
The casements, by rain in profusion on the glass.

71

We will never say a grief remains the same
In the velvet parlor as it exists by the lake
In utter stillness or expresses itself
On the road driven past ditches of spring flowers.

Being aware of these facts,
We must remember when the poem is read
To be on the west side of the mountain,
To have our backs to a red sky, to read
From the page held high in black silhouette
Beside a full pine.

THE SUCCESS OF THE HUNT

> There was a white hart that lived in that forest, and if anyone
> killed it, he would be hanged. . . .—*My Antonia*

He was sighted once in a clearing at dusk, the gold
Grass up to his shoulders and he standing like a pillar
Of salt staring back; seen again from a high ledge,
A motionless dot of white curled like a bloom
In the green below; surprised along a lake shore
At night, taken for an irregular reflection
Of the moon on the surf.

Some looked only for his red eyes, believing
The body could be too easily hidden
By the translucent green of lighted leaves,
That it could sink blue below the water
Or become boundless against the snow, almost invisible,
That it was not white at night.

Some who followed what was presumed to be his trail
Found the purple toadflax said to grow only
From his hoof marks, and some became engulfed
By cecropia moths thought to spring from his urine.
Others testified to the impassable white cliffs
Alleged to be an accumulated battery of his shadows.

Those who lost their way were forced to rediscover
The edible buds of the winter spruce, and to use
The fronds of the cycas for warmth, to repeat again
To themselves the directional details of moss,
And part the pampas grasses clear to the earth,
To smell their way east.

But those who followed furthest with the most detail,
Who actually saw the water rising in his hoof prints
And touched the trees still moist where their bark
Had been stripped, those who recognized at the last moment
The prongs of his antlers disappearing over the edge

73

Of their vision, they were the ones who learned to tell
By the imbalance of their feet on the earth where it was
He slept at night and by their own vertigo how it was he rose
To nip the dogwood twigs above his head. They learned to smell
His odor in their bedclothes and to waken suddenly at night
To the silence of his haunches rubbing on the ash.
Even now they can find the spot where he walked
From the water dripping and trace on their palms
The path of his winter migration. They can isolate
From any direction the eight lighted points
Of his antlers imprinted in the night sky.
And these, who were methodical with the most success,
Always meant to do more than murder.

PART IV

A Giant Has Swallowed the Earth

What will it do for him, to have internalized
The many slender stems of riverlets and funnels,
The blunt toes of the pine cone fallen, to have ingested
Lakes in gold slabs at dawn and the peaked branches
Of the fir under snow? He has taken into himself
The mist of the hazel nut, the white hairs of the moth,
And the mole's velvet snout. He remembers, by inner
Voice alone, fogs over frozen grey marshes, fine
Salt on the blunt of the cliff.

What will it mean to him to perceive things
First from within—the mushroom's fold, the martin's
Tongue, the spotted orange of the wallaby's ear,
To become the object himself before he comprehends it,
Putting into perfect concept without experience
The din of the green gully in spring mosses?

And when he stretches on his bed and closes his eyes,
What patterns will appear to him naturally—the schematic
Tracings of the Vanessa butterfly in migration, tacks
And red strings marking the path of each mouse
In the field, nucleic chromosomes aligning their cylinders
In purple before their separation? The wind must settle
All that it carries behind his face and rise again
In his vision like morning.

A giant has swallowed the earth,
And when he sleeps now, o when he sleeps,
How his eyelids murmur, how we envy his dream.

THE SIGNIFICANCE OF LOCATION

The cat has the chance to make the sunlight
Beautiful, to stop it and turn it immediately
Into black fur and motion, to take it
As shifting branch and brown feather
Into the back of the brain forever.

The cardinal has flown the sun in red
Through the oak forest to the lawn.,
The finch has caught it in yellow
And taken it among the thorns. By the spider
It has been bound tightly and tied
In an eight-stringed knot.

The sun has been intercepted in its one
Basic state and changed to a million varieties
Of green stick and tassle. It has been broken
Into pieces by glass rings, by mist
Over the river. Its heat
Has been given the board fence for body,
The desert rock for fact. On winter hills
It has been laid down in white like a martyr.

This afternoon we could spread gold scarves
Clear across the field and say in truth,
"Sun you are silk."

Imagine the sun totally isolated,
Its brightness shot in continuous streaks straight out
Into the black, never arrested,
Never once being made light.

Someone should take note
Of how the earth has saved the sun from oblivion.

COUNTING WHAT THE CACTUS CONTAINS

Elf owl, cactus wren, fruit flys incubating
In the only womb they'll ever recognize.
Shadow for the sand rat, spines
And barbary ribs clenched with green wax.
Seven thousand thorns, each a water slide,
A wooden tongue licking the air dry.

Inside, early morning mist captured intact,
The taste of drizzle sucked
And sunsplit. Whistle
Of the red-tailed hawk at midnight, rush
Of the leaf-nosed bat, the soft slip
Of fog easing through sand held in tandem.

Counting, the vertigo of its attitudes
Across the evening; in the wood of its latticed bones—
The eye sockets of every saint of thirst;
In the gullet of each night-blooming flower—the crucifix
Of the arid.

In its core, a monastery of cells, a brotherhood
Of electrons, a column of expanding darkness
Where matter migrates and sparks whorl
And travel has no direction, where distance
Bends backward over itself and the ascension
Of Venus, the stability of Polaris, are crucial.

The cactus, containing
Whatever can be said to be there,
Plus the measurable tremble of its association
With all those who have been counting.

Making a History

The glutinous snail
In silvery motion
Has rubbed his neck
Against his mate's, covered
Her side-slatted orifice
With his own. The newt,
Jumping suddenly forward underwater,
Has twisted and dropped
His pocket of sperm. And in the field
The fritillary, frenzied for orange,
Has skittered straight up and hovered.

The chortle of the Siamese fighting fish
Held upside down by her mate
Has subsided. The dragon fish
Has chewed the tail of his lover,
And the frigate has been swollen
Three times, burgeoning in red.
Bison have risen from their dirt clouds
Blowing. Antlers have entangled, caribou
Collided, cockerels have caught hold,
And the crack of the mountain sheep meeting
Has broken over the arroyo, and the bowerbirds
Have howled and the fruit bats screamed,
And the wild pigs have lain down
In punctuated barking, and the zig-zag cocking
Of the stickleback has widened, and alligators
Have spit and strumped, thrashing
In the crumpled reeds. Storks have bent backward
Rooting at heaven with their long beaks banging,
And the alley cat, in guttural moaning,
Has finally been released, bleeding
At the neck, and everyone
Has something to remember.

FINDING THE FIRE LINE

Storks precede grass fires
On the Serengeti, snapping up small
Fleeing reptiles.

If I state a location—
In the middle of the Mojave Desert at dusk,
In the core of the cathedral cactus,
Bound by the fragrance of dark milk—
I have partially described whatever must be there.

Gordon read aloud, "Wounded soldiers
In long grey coats came to the house all night,
And I gave the first one my bed."

Gordon doesn't know whether smoke on the Serengeti
Is grass partially read aloud or the dark
Fragrance of whatever the storks have predicted.
Will lizards fleeing the fire line
Find whatever must be totally defined
In the center of the beak's bed?
By describing the wounds preceding them,
Those who move toward the middle
Of the long grey dusk can be located.

PORTRAIT

This is a picture of you
Reading this poem. Concentrate
On the finite movement
Of your eyes as they travel
At this moment across
The page, your fingers
Maintaining the stability
Of the sheet. Focus on the particular
Fall of your hair, the scent
Of your hands, the placement of your
Feet now as they acknowledge
Their name.

Simultaneously with these words, be aware
Of your tongue against
Your teeth, the aura
Of heat at your neckline
And wrists, the sense
Of your breath inside its own hollows.

Imagine yourself
Ten feet away and look back
At your body positioned
Here with this book. Picture
The perspective, the attitude
Of your shoulders and hips,
The bend of your head as you
Read of yourself.

Watch how you turn back as you
Remember the sounds surrounding you now,
As you recall the odors
Of wood fibers in this place
Or the lack of them.

And take note of this part
Of your portrait—the actual
Mechanism by which you are perceiving
The picture, the fixed
Expression on your face as you
Arrange these words at this moment
Into their proper circles, as you
Straighten out the aspects
Of the page, the linguistics of the sight
And color of light on the paper.

This is the printed
Form of you watching
Yourself now as you consider
Your person. This portrait is
Finished when you raise
Your eyes.

Seeing the Glory

Whatever enters the eye—shade of ash leaf,
Torn web dangling, movement of ice
Over the canyon edge—enters only
As the light of itself.
It travels through the clear jelly
Of the vitreo, turning once like the roll
Of a fish in deep water, causing a shimmer
In that thimbleful of cells waiting,
Then proceeds as a quiver on a dark purple thread
To pass from life into recognition.

The trick is to perceive glory
When its light enters the eye,
To recognize its penetration of the lens
Whether it comes like the sudden crack
Of glass shot or the needle in the center
Of the hailstone, whether it appears like the slow
Parting of fog by steady trees or the flashing
Of piranha at their prey.

How easily it could go unnoticed
Existing unseen as that line initiating
The distinction of all things.
It must be called by name
Whether it dives with triple wings of gold
Before the optic nerve or presses itself
In black fins against the retina
Or rises in its inversion like a fish
Breaking into sky.

Watching on this hillside tonight,
I want to know how to see
And bear witness.

ON THE EXISTENCE OF THE SOUL

How confident I am it is there. Don't I bring it,
As if it were enclosed in a fine leather case,
To particular places solely for its own sake?
Haven't I set it down before the variegated canyon
And the undeviating bald salt dome?
Don't I feed it on ivory calcium and ruffled
Shell bellies, shore boulders, on the sight
Of the petrel bird motionless over the sea, its splayed
Feet hanging? Don't I make sure it apprehends
The invisibly fine spray more than once?

I have seen that it takes in every detail
I can manage concerning the garden wall and its borders.
I have listed for it the comings and goings
Of one hundred species of insects explicitly described.
I have named the chartreuse stripe
And the fimbriated antenna, the bulbed thorax
And the multiple eye. I have sketched
The brilliant wings of the trumpet vine and invented
New vocabularies describing the interchanges between rocks
And their crevices, between the holly lip
And its concept of itself.

And if not for its sake, why would I go
Out into the night alone and stare deliberately
Straight up into 15 billion years ago and more?

I have cherished it. I have named it.
By my own solicitations
I have proof of its presence.

SYNTHESIZING THE WORD

The speckled wood butterfly guards his spot of light
On the forest floor. He rests in that circle of sun
Like a powdery flower against the earth, sounding
Its fragrances. He flies in a spiral upward
Against usurpers, settles again on everything good
That he can distinguish. I am trying to find
Your name. I am trying to remember.

In the field after dark, everything has a sound,
The damp gathering under the weeds, the shift
Of the comb-footed spider, the edges of the trees
Against the night. I am aware of what moves across the tops
Of the grasses and keeps on going. I attend to the pauses
Of the grape-skin peepers, the pine crickets. I am trying
To recall your name. I am watching.

The wild wheat, evening-brown and counting, rises
And bends in the ditches by the road. The other side
Of its existence is here in these words. The hair
Of each seed-head, the invisible crack in each sheath,
The wind taking form among the stalks, all have been here
On this page waiting for themselves from the beginning.
I will put together your name. I am adding.

Reminiscence of barn owls and tit-toms, filaments of jackanapes
And iris bands, auras of glassed-in candlelight and unbroken
Spans of snow, the underwater worm slides along the body
Of the Choctaw reed, feeling its presence. I am
Next to where you are. I will use my fingertips. I will use
My belly. I will study long enough to remember your name.

The Literary Man

He isn't a curiosity, merely an object
Of study. If he reads these words, "the castle
On the hill," he sees immediately the block
Fortress, the greystone turrets, wooden gate.
Each detail is as real as the paper he holds—
The mossy foundation, the weed-filled grasses.

Show him this grouping of letters: "Red poppies
And purple iris grow by the crumbling wall." He has
No trouble. Or: "All night long he kept his hand
On her thigh." It might just as well have happened.

This is not so remarkable. We shouldn't be amazed.
But he told me yesterday that if your name
Were spelled differently you wouldn't be the same.
And today on the beach he saw—entirely present there
And as recognizable as the spread of their wings—
The word "gulls" at the same instant as he saw the birds.
"Flight" and "swoop" appeared with their maneuvers,
And printed in among them as if a plane trailed
A banner, "S-C-R-E-E! S-C-R-E-E!"

He says he would be blind, wouldn't recognize
This fruit on my table at all, if he didn't
See "apple" at the same moment, and the fruit
Responds by becoming so nearly "apple" that the name
Is tighter to it than its own stretched and grown-on
Red skin. He says you could cut it in half and the two
"p's" would be split down the middle staring back at you.

Elm becomes different merely by becoming "elm,"
And he challenges you to identify the tree outside your window
Right now without seeing, in that fraction of a second
When you know that you know it, the word that is its name.

By Hearing the Same Story Over and Over

Some things can be established and then forgotten,
For instance—the general area above is always occupied
By sky; the overall sense of the forest never depends
On a particular tree; light is itself only up to the perimeters
Of darkness.

One is left then to concentrate on details.
You might not have realized before how the sun
Never clears the haze from the meadow until the pine trees
Draw their shadows into their trunks at noon,
And the connection between the dry southwestern wind
And the toad caches dug in on the northeastern slopes
Might seem suddenly obvious on the sixth reading.
The violet butterfly keeping pace with the dry leaf shuffle
Of the villain all the way through the forest
Must have been here unseen all along.

Learning to know the story by heart, you might wonder
How events are altered by being anticipated.
What happens to the momentum of the rock scheduled
To crash by surprise down the hillside
When its fall is seen in expectation five minutes before
It begins to move? And how does it affect the clear air
Over the valley when you can smell smoke
From the Indians' fire two days before their camp
Comes into existence? There is no doubt, you come,
By these means, to believe in endings before they happen.

Occasionally you embellish the story yourself.
Your wish on the 20th reading for a clear lake hidden
In reflective black beneath the ledge where the hero
Waits, means it is there, complete with surface beetles
And shore decay, in somebody's eyes for a moment.
And your desire to be the one who rides with the lawman
This time through the thick poplars means you might discover,
Without its being written, that branches can slap hard

While still remaining stationary. Your growing love
Of the hero's aspect in boots must draw his body,
As if he breathed, nearer to actuality.

On the 100th reading after you have seen once more
How the hero binds the wrists of the villain
And have noticed for the first time the ingenuity
Of that knot and after you have said to yourself
As they disappear into the town, "termination,"
Then when you turn back to start at the beginning again
It might occur to you to ask why the sky must always
Occupy the same general area above. You might be struck
By the singular notion that the overall sense of the forest
Must always depend on every particular tree. And light,
You know by the details of your own anticipated embellishments,
Can be itself only by never accepting the perimeters
Of any darkness.

ALL THE ELEMENTS OF THE SCENE

In the upper righthand corner of this scene is a copse
Of cottonwood (populus deltoides). Each leaf
Like a silver dollar twists on its flattened stalk.
And parallel to the edge of this scene runs
A line of forest, thin dwarf oak, scrub vine,
The smoketree. Leaning to the left of that, a field
Of flat grasses sways, heavy with thorny seeds. Blue
Toadflax and beebalm bend in the wind toward
The bare rim of the pond in the foreground, its lazy
Wash surfaced with the baweedle bug, the raised eyes
Of the leopard frog (rana pipiens). Pickerelweeds
Make hostage of the dragonfly, the nesting mud tortoise.

Here am I in this scene too, my shadow wrinkling
On the water of the pond, my footprints making pools
Along the bank. And all that I say, each word
That I give to this scene is part of the scene. The act
Of each thing identified being linked to its name
Becomes an object itself here. The bumblebee hovers
Near the bitter orange of the mallow weed. That sentence
And this one too are elements of the scene.

This poem, as real as the carp sliding in green
At the bottom of the pond, is the only object
Within the scene capable of discussing both itself
And the scene. The moist, rotting log sinks
Into earth. The pink toothwort sprouts beside it.
The poem of this scene has 34 lines.

And see, reader, you are here also, watching
As the poem speaks to you, as it points out that you
Were present at the very first word. The fact of your
Cognizance here is established as you read this sentence.

90

Take note of the existence of the words in this scene
As they tell you—the pond is purple; the sun is blocked
In branches below the oak; there are shadows
On this poem; night things are stirring.

THAT SONG

I will use the cormorant on his rope at night diving
Into the sea, and the fire on the prow, and the fish
Like ribbons sliding toward the green light in the dark.

I will remember the baneberry and the bladderwort
And keep the white crone under the bosackle tree
And the translucent figs and the candelabra burning alone
In the middle of the plains, and the twig girdler,
And the lizard of Christ running over the waves.

I will take the egg bubble on the flute
Of the elm and the ministries of the predacious
Caul beetle, the spit of the iris, the red juice shot
From the eye of the horny toad, and I will use
The irreducible knot wound by the hazel scrub
And the bog myrtle still tangling, and the sea horse
With his delicate horn, the flywheel of his maneuvering.

I will remember exactly each tab folded down
In the sin book of Sister Alleece and each prayer
Hanging in its painted cylinder above the door
And the desert goat at noon facing
The sun to survive.

I will include the brindled bandicoot and the barnacle
Goose and the new birds hatching from mussels
Under the sea and the migrating wildebeests humming
Like organs, moaning like men.

The sand swimmers alive under the Gobi plateau,
The cactus wren in her nest of thorns and the herald
Of the tarantula wasp and each yellow needle
In the spring field rising, everything will be there,
And nothing will be wasted.

THE LITERARY ADVENTURE

At the exact moment that you begin to read this, a wasp
In the Kalahari Desert appears at the top
Of a large sand hill. Understand how she stops,
Spotting her prey, the crystal sand spider. Alerted,
The spider turns to fight, rising up on his white legs, striking
With rapid blows the blue-black body of the wasp
As she darts forward. He retreats,
Forms an eight-spoked cartwheel and spins
Wildly down the sand.

As you read these lines, she follows quickly,
Catches him on his back by his crystal legs
And straddles his body. The needle of her poison
Tube sinks slowly into the golden raisin
Of his abdomen. She remains poised until he rests.

If you continue, she begins to burrow, throwing
Sand with a fine whisking of her feet. There is a clatter
And dry careening of small rocks and gravel as she kicks
The refuse behind her.

Proceeding down the page: she drags
His heavy body to her tunnel, stuffs it
With the pins of her legs deep into the hole.
His feet draw together at the top like a stringed
Purse. His mandibles, his multiple eyes are frozen.

When you conceive the oval of this word, she
Places her egg like a glistening snowdrop
On the spider's pulsing frame, climbs out,
Turns backward, fills the hole to the top.

Look at this stanza. In the orange sun
She is combing the dust from her double wings.

As you finish this sentence to the end, she hurries away,
Head lowered, the practiced wires of her body
Disappearing with the alacrity of the very small,
Over the edge of the broad evening dune.

NASA Takes a 63-Year-Old Poet to the First Space Station

Finally ready, they come for him at dawn.
Touching each elbow, they surround him carefully
Like a porcelain vase. They have a car waiting.
He needs no special suit, his gabardine pants,
Flannel shirt, khaki tie. They are pleased
With his fingertips, the creases in his shoes.

Into the gleaming shuttlecraft, they lead him
To his room. All of his walls are wide
Circular windows facing forward, his ceiling,
A skylight. He settles on pillows
In his high-domed cubicle of glass.

The rise is perfect, silent, without tremor.
He is carried up through the early grey
Fog of the eastern seaboard, out over
The earth, an enormous belly of blue.
Far ahead he sees the massive construct floating,
The pristine exactness of its white metal, silver
Girders, wired columns of crosses
And mirrored wheels turning slowly.

As he watches, sped forward into the cloudless
And the snow-silent, into the blue-black hollow,
Into the dust-free, spit-and-polished starlight
Of the nethermost,
They hand him his pencil and pad.

THE FEAR OF FALLING

It comes from the tree apes, this instinct
To grasp, to fill the hollow of the hand
And fasten. Emerging from the womb,
How each must have clawed, grabbing before breathing,
Its mother's hairy knee, the slip of her rump.
Imagine the weak, the unimpressed, dropping
Through leaves like stones to the ground below.

The mind has become itself inside the panic
Of bodies falling with fingers spread useless.
How many times in the jerk of sleep
Has the last hand-hold been seen
Disappearing upward like a small bird sucked into space?

Bound to the clenching habit of the fingers, united
With the compulsion of the hands to grasp, the mind
Perceives in terms of possession, recognizing
Its lack from the beginning—the black fur
Of the void, the bowl of the wide belly, the dark
Of that great invented thigh out of reach.

The first need of the brain is to curl
The conceptual knuckles and tighten.
And whether it is on each warm-water crack
At the bottom of the sea or on every maneuver
Of the swamp muskrat or around the grey spiral
Details of forgiveness, the grip of the brain
Is determined not to be negligible.

Here in the wind at the top of these branches
We recognize
The persistent need to take hold of something
Known to be sure-footed.

Capturing the Scene

With pen and ink, the artist takes care
To be explicit, each board of the covered bridge
Elucidated, each shingle of the roof. The columns
Of the termites and the holes of the borers to be,
He remembers. He is deliberate to denote those specifics
He understands, filling in the blank with the pause
Of the dragonfly, the scratch of the myrtle weed.
He watches to maintain in his lines exactly
That tedious balance between the river in motion
And the river itself. Like wires, he coordinates
The trees and their affinity for disorder.

How skillfully he locates the woodthrush clearing
The last field beyond the hills, and the worn rocks
Along the bank, each with its own specific hump
Against space. He acknowledges the sunken
And the sucked away, the shadows on the far left
Bearing witness to objects still outside the scene.

And notice how he achieves that incandescence of ink
Around the seed pod. He knows that the scream of the jay,
The odor of the sun-dried wood is entirely in his stroke.
Without making a single mark, he executes the heavens.

And hasn't he understood from the beginning where he must never
Look directly—into the dark hedgerow on the opposite bank,
Among the crossed sticks of the rushes and the spaces between,
How he must not stare steadily at the long fall
Of the sky below the horizon or probe too deeply that area
Lying between the ink and its line on the paper? He knows
There is that which he must draw blindfolded or not at all.
And before he can give to the scene its final name,
He must first identify every facet of its multiplicity
In detail; he must then turn away his face completely
And remember more.